Albin Marine Engines O-11, O-21, O-41, O-411

Instruction Book

Albin Marine Engines O-11, O-21, O-41, O-411

Instruction Book

ISBN/EAN: 9783954275021
Erscheinungsjahr: 2012
Erscheinungsort: Bremen, Deutschland

© maritimepress in Europäischer Hochschulverlag GmbH & Co. KG, Fahrenheitstr. 1, 28359 Bremen. Alle Rechte beim Verlag und bei den jeweiligen Lizenzgebern.

www.maritimepress.de | office@maritimepress.de

Bei diesem Titel handelt es sich um den Nachdruck eines historischen, lange vergriffenen Buches. Da elektronische Druckvorlagen für diese Titel nicht existieren, musste auf alte Vorlagen zurückgegriffen werden. Hieraus zwangsläufig resultierende Qualitätsverluste bitten wir zu entschuldigen.

INSTRUCTION BOOK

ALBIN Marine Engines

O-11, O-21, O-41 and O-411

Before you run your new engine, we recommend you to study this instruction book carefully. It contains all the necessary advice you will need for running and maintaining the engine correctly. if you note the advice and instructions given, we are confident that the performance and running economy will be all that you may expect of a quality product.

ALBIN

ALBIN O-11

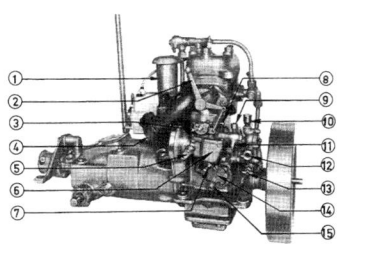

Fig. 1

1 Connection for cooling water thermometer
2 Temperature control *)
3 Drain cock for crankcase water jacket
4 Oil dipstick for crankcase
5 Reverse gear lever
6 Threeway cock for cooling water
7 Cooling water discharge
8 Magneto
9 Oil dipstick for reverse gear
10 Propeller shaft coupling
11 Oil drain plug for reverse gear

*) fitted to engine without thermostat cooling.

Fig. 2

1 Oil filler pipe
2 Throttle lever
3 Idling adjustment screw
4 Exhaust manifold
5 Choke lever
6 Carburettor
7 Drain screw for float chamber
8 Mixture control screw
9 Connection for oil pressure gauge
10 Grease cup for cooling water pump
11 Connection for fuel pipe
12 Cooling water pump suction intake
13 Drain cock for cooling water pump
14 Oil pump
15 Relief valve for oil pump

ALBIN O-21

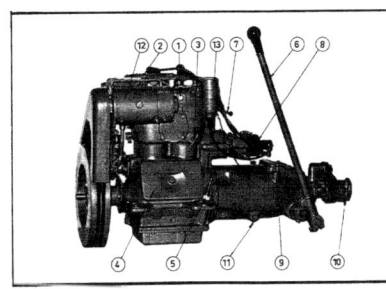

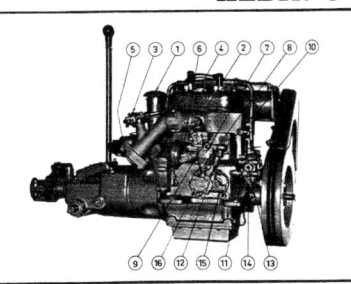

Fig. 3

1 Connection for cooling water thermometer
2 Thermostat
3 Drain cock for crankcase water jacket
4 Crankcase inspection cover
5 Oil dipstick for crankcase
6 Reverse gear lever
7 Cooling water discharge
8 Distributor
9 Oil dipstick for reverse gear
10 Propeller shaft coupling
11 Oil drain plug for reverse gear
12 Dynastarter
13 Ignition coil

Fig. 4

1 Oil filler pipe
2 Throttle lever
3 Threeway cock for cooling water
4 Idling adjustment screw
5 Exhaust pipe connection
6 Choke lever
7 Carburettor
8 Drain screw for float chamber
9 Mixture control screw
10 Connection for fuel pipe
11 Grease cup for cooling water pump
12 Connection for oil pressure gauge
13 Cooling water pump suction intake
14 Drain cock for cooling water pump
15 Relief valve for oil pump
16 Oil pump

ALBIN O-41

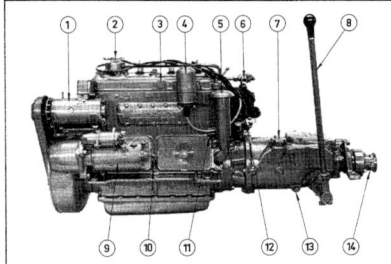

Fig. 7
1. Generator
2. Thermostat
3. Connection for cooling water thermometer
4. Ignition coil
5. Oil filler pipe
6. Cooling water discharge
7. Oil filler cap for reverse gear
8. Reverse gear lever
9. Starter
10. Oil dipstick for crankcase
11. Drain cock for crankcase water jacket
12. Distributor
13. Oil drain plug for reverse gear
14. Propeller shaft coupling

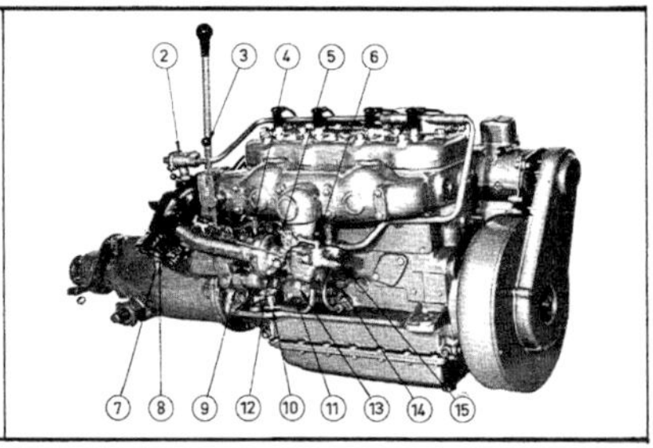

Fig. 8
2. Threeway cock for cooling water
3. Throttle lever
4. Drain cock for exhaust manifold jacket
5. Idling adjustment screw
6. Mixture control screw
7. Oil dipstick in reverse gear
8. Exhaust pipe connection
9. Cooling water pump suction intake
10. Drain cock for cooling water pump
11. Oil pump
12. Choke lever
13. Drain screw for float chamber
14. Connection for oil pressure gauge
15. Connection for fuel pipe

ALBIN O-411

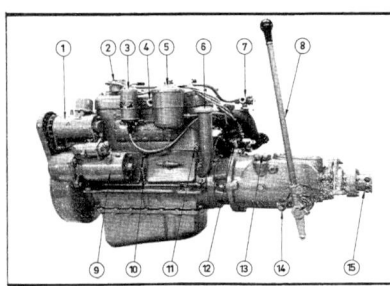

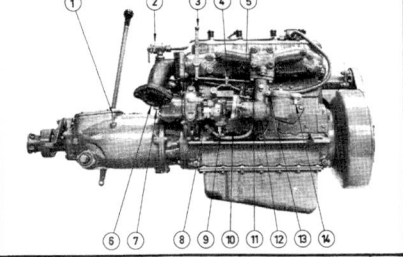

Fig. 9
1. Generator
2. Thermostat
3. Ignition coil
4. Connection for cooling water thermometer
5. Lubricating oil filter
6. Oil filler pipe
7. Cooling water discharge
8. Reverse gear lever
9. Starter
10. Oil dipstick for crankcase
11. Drain cock for crankcase water jacket
12. Distributor
13. Oil filler cap for reverse gear
14. Oil drain plug for reverse gear
15. Propeller shaft coupling

Fig. 10
1. Oil dipstick for reverse gear
2. Threeway cock for cooling water
3. Throttle lever
4. Drain cock for exhaust manifold water jacket
5. Choke lever
6. Exhaust pipe connection
7. Grease cup for distributor gear housing
8. Cooling water pump suction intake
9. Drain cock for cooling water pump
10. Oil pump
11. Idling adjustment screw
12. Connection for oil pressure gauge
13. Mixture control screw
14. Connection for fuel pipe

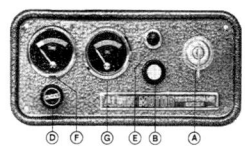

Fig. 11 Instrument panel
A Switch box
B Starter button
D Choke
E Charging control light
F Water temperature gauge
G Oil pressure gauge

STARTING AND RUNNING

Running-in

When a new engine leaves the factory it has already been partly run-in and has been carefully checked and bench-tested up to the specified output. It is recommended that the engine be run at only half throttle for the first 25 hours in order to complete the running-in process. Thereafter, the load may be progressively increased. Careful running-in is of vital importance for the length of life and reliable performance of the engine.

Before starting

1 Open the engine cover so that the engine compartment is properly ventilated. Pump out the bilge water carefully and check at the same time that no fuel leakage has occurred.

2 Use the oil dipstick on the port side of the engine to check the lubricating oil level in the crankcase. When necessary, fill up with lubricating oil to the upper level mark on the dipstick. Use lubricating oil having quality Service MM of the viscosity SAE 30 during summer and SAE 20 during winter.

3 Check the lubricating oil level in the reverse gear. Use the special oil dipstick intended for this purpose. When necessary, fill oil up to the level mark. Use oil of the same make and quality as in the engine.

4 Lubricate the cooling water pump by turning the grease cup one turn. NOTE! Avoid over lubrication, as there is a risk that grease may penetrate into the cooling system. Use multi-purpose water-pump grease.

5 Grease the propeller shaft bearings. Use multi-purpose water-pump grease.

6 Check that the cooling water drain cocks on the engine block and the cooling water pump are closed. Open the sea-cock for the cooling water intake.

7 Check that the threeway cock for the cooling water outlet is adjusted for discharge overboard. NOTE. When a heat resistant rubber exhaust hose is used all the cooling water must be fed through the exhaust system at all times. The rubber exhaust hose will otherwise become damaged due to overheating.

8 Check the fuel level in the tank and open the fuel cock. If the engine is a petrol/paraffin model, the threeway cock should be switched over to petrol (gasoline). At the same time, check pipes and fittings for fuel leakage.

Starting

1 Set the reverse gear lever to neutral.
2 On engines with electrical equipment insert the ignition key.
3 Set the throttle control to one-third open.
4 Close the choke and crank the engine round a few times. Then open the choke (in cold weather).
5 Start the engine by cranking or, if it has electrical equipment, by pressing the starter button.

If the engine has received too rich a mixture due to excessive choking, it will be necessary to set the throttle to "full" before the engine will start.

The starting procedure varies with individual engines, so that it may be necessary to modify the above instructions accordingly.

After starting

1 Set the magneto ignition control to "advance". (Only for engines with magneto ignition.)
2 Check the cooling water circulation.

3 Set the threeway cock on the exhaust manifold to the middle position.

NOTE. When a heat resistant rubber exhaust hose is used all the cooling water must be fed through the exhaust system at all times. The rubber exhaust hose will otherwise become damaged due to overheating.

4 Check the oil pressure.

Manoeuvring

Move the gearbox lever forward for running ahead and aft for running astern. When manoeuvring, the engine should be running slowly. Sharp jerking of the lever will cause unnecessary strain on the engine and reverse gear. Excessively slow movement of the lever can cause the clutch to slip. When shifting the lever from ahead or astern to neutral, adjust the throttle to avoid racing the engine.

Running

When running, check the engine oil pressure and cooling water temperature at regular intervals. If the engine has electrical equipment also note whether the battery is charging. The charging control light glows when the ignition is switched on and at low revolutions but is extinguished at high revolutions, which indicates that the dynamo is charging. In the case of petrol/paraffin models the threeway fuel cock should not be switched over to paraffin (kerosene) until the engine has reached full operating temperature, i.e. about $80°$ C ($166°$ F) - the temperature indicator within the green area of the cooling water thermometer. In order to obtain good combustion when running on paraffin (kerosene), the engine should not be run below half load, nor below half throttle, except for short periods. Before stopping the engine, switch over to petrol (gasoline) in good time in order to facilitate restarting. If the engine should stop unexpectedly while

ALBIN O-11 COMBI

running on paraffin (kerosene), drain the carburettor through the drain cock provided before moving the threeway fuel cock over to petrol (gasoline).

Experience has shown that the octane rating of paraffin (kerosene) available on the market sometimes varies. This may result in knocking when running on one particular brand of paraffin (kerosene), although the engine may run perfectly well on other brands. In such cases, the knocking can be eliminated by mixing 15 - 25% of petrol (gasoline) with the paraffin (kerosene).

Stopping

1 Switch the threeway cock to petrol (gasoline). (Only in the case of paraffin (kerosene) running.)

2 Move the threeway cock for the cooling water outlet to discharge overboard (about 1/2 minute before stopping the engine).
NOTE. When a heat resistant rubber exhaust hose is used all the cooling water must be fed through the exhaust system at all times. The rubber exhaust hose will otherwise become damaged due to overheating.

3 Switch off the ignition.

4 Close the fuel cock.

SPECIAL ADVICE AND INSTRUCTIONS FOR O-11 COMBI AND O-21 COMBI

Starting

When starting the engine the remote control lever should be in neutral position. In summer choking of the engine is not normally required.

If the engine is used in early spring or late autumn it may be necessary to use the choke. The remote control lever should be in neutral position. When the choke control is pulled out, the throttle butterfly will automatically open resulting in an increased idling speed. As soon as the engine is warm, push in the choke control.

Running

Move the remote control lever forward for running ahead and aft for running astern. When the control lever is moved forward the propeller pitch as well as the speed of the engine is increased in correct proportions. The same happens when the control lever is moved aft from the neutral position.

To achieve less possible drag from the propeller when sailing, it can be feathered by moving the control lever as far aft as possible.

When running ahead the engine speed can be too low if the control lever has been moved too far ahead. This can happen in rough sea or if the engine is installed in a particularly big boat. However, the control lever should be set in a position giving the engine a speed of about 1450 rpm.

Lubrication (Combi)

It is particularly important that the manoeuvring mechanism is lubricated at least once every season. When lubricating proceed as follows: Set the remote control lever in neutral position. Pump in grease through the pressure lubricating nipple on the manoeuvring mechanism - at least 20 pump strokes. The pressure lubricating nipple is located on the port side.

Lubricate with a suitable grease for the application - we recommend Shell Alvania EP 2 or Esso Beacon 2.

The cam curve of the manoeuvring mechanism should also be lubricated with the same type of grease. The ball joint and also the fork end connection for the teleflex device should be lubricated with ordinary thin oil.

ALBIN O-21 COMBI

MAINTENANCE SCHEME

		Daily	Every 50 hours 1)	Every 250 hours 1)
1	Check the oil level in the engine, reverse gear and reduction gear	x		
2	Turn the grease cup for the cooling water pump about one turn	x 2)		
3	Change the engine oil		x	
4	Clean the oil filler cap breather (only 0-11)			x
5	Change the oil in the reverse gear and reduction gear			x
6	Check the spark plugs			x
7	Clean the fuel filter and carburettor			x
8	Check the contact breaker points			x
9	Check the dynastart V-belt tension		x	
10	Check the acid level of the battery	x		
11	Check the charging condition of the battery		x	
12	General inspection and overhaul of the engine, reverse gear and electric equipment			3)

1) Alternatively once every season if this time interval is reached first.
2) Every 10 hours.
3) Whenever necessary or, for example, every other year.

10

LUBRICATING SYSTEM

The lower part of the crankcase acts as an oil reservoir. The oil quantity for the different engine types is: 0-11 0.5 litres (0.88 Imp. pints/1.05 US pints), 0-21 1.4 litres (2.46 Imp.pints/2.95 US pints), 0-41 3.3 litres (5.8 Imp. pints/6.97 US pints), and 0-411 5.0 litres (8.8 Imp. pints/10.56 US pints). The engine is filled with oil through the filler pipe and the level checked with the dipstick. Use engine oil with the quality Service MM. During summer the viscosity should be SAE 30 and during winter SAE 20.

A gear pump circulates the lubricating oil. The oil pressure is set at the factory and indicated on a gauge. Normal pressure is in the green section of the gauge. When the engine is warm and run at normal speed, the oil pressure should be 1.5 - 2.5 kg/cm^2 (20 - 35 p.s.i.). A discrepancy in the pressure may be a sign of a defect in the lubrication system, which must then be examined thoroughly.

With a new engine, the oil should be changed after the first 25 hours running and thereafter every 50 hours. The old oil is drained through the drain plug on the crankcase. If this is not accessible, the oil is removed by sucking it out through the dipstick hole with a special suction pump included in the tool kit. Always change the oil after laying up (e.g. winter lay-up), regardless of how little the oil has been used.

The engine type 0-11 has a breather on the oil filler cap (fig. 12). Check that the breather ball A does not stick but works satisfactorily. The ball valve should be washed in petrol (gasoline).

The engine 0-411 is provided with a "Fram" lubricating oil filter. The filter element should be changed every 150 hours - cleaning the old element is not recommended. The element can be replaced by simply removing the cover of the filter body. Clean the body and fit new seals which are supplied with the element when replacing the unit. After reassembling run the engine until warm and check that there is no leakage - especially from the seal between the filter body and its cover.

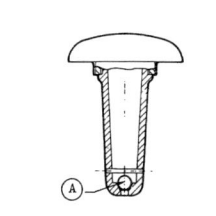

Fig. 12

Oil filler cap with sectional view of breather (0-11).

A Breather ball

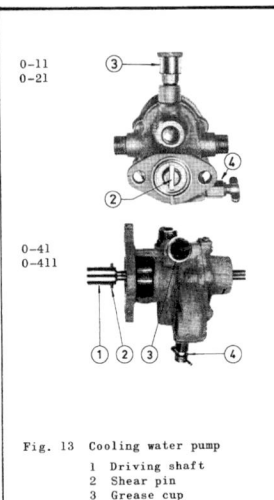

Fig. 13 Cooling water pump
1 Driving shaft
2 Shear pin
3 Grease cup
4 Drain cock

0-11
0-21

0-41
0-411

COOLING SYSTEM

The cooling water is circulated in the engine water passages by means of a gear pump. The pump drive from the camshaft is transmitted through a shear pin, which is made of special material as a safety measure. If the pump has frozen during cold weather or seized for some other reason, the shear pin will break when the engine starts, thus preventing damage to the pump. A spare shear pin should be held in reserve and can be fitted by removing the cooling water pump.

The cooling water pump should be lubricated every 10 hours during running by turning the grease cup fitted on the pump about one turn. Use water-resistant grease. Make sure that the lubricating cup is filled with grease and lubricate by gradually screwing down the cup. Over-greasing should be avoided as the excess grease will enter the pump and be passed, together with water, into the cooling water jackets where it will be deposited on the wall, thus impairing the circulation.

Before starting set the cooling water threeway cock to direct discharge so that all the water passes out through the pipe overboard. This makes it easy to check that the circulation is satisfactory. After this, set the cock to its middle position. The water will then be discharged partly through the overboard pipe and partly through the exhaust pipe. The water passing through the exhaust cools this pipe and deadens the exhaust noise. About ½ minute prior to stopping, set the threeway cock to discharge overboard again so that the exhaust gases will blow the pipe free from water and from steam.

NOTE. When a heat resistant rubber exhaust hose is used all the cooling water must be fed through the exhaust system at all times. The rubber exhaust hose will otherwise become damaged due to overheating.

The cooling water discharge should be located about one foot above the waterline.

The working temperature is of great importance to the length of life, fuel economy, smooth running and general functioning of the engine. Therefore the engines are provided with a thermostat which automatically keeps the engine temperature correct independent of load and temperature of the entering water.

The thermostat, which is placed in the cylinder head, is of the bellows type. Should the bellows fail to operate correctly the thermostat will remain open and the engine temperature will be correspondingly lower. After having removed the thermostat housing from the cylinder head, the thermostat can easily be changed.

Engines with handstart have a thermometer which is fitted in the cylinder head. With this type of thermometer the cooling water temperature shall be within the white section.

Engines with electric equipment have the cooling water temperature gauge fitted in the instrument panel. With this type of thermometer the temperature shall be within the green section.

When fitting the cooling water temperature gauge make sure that the capillary tube is adequately supported. The tube should be supported close to the instrument, as shown in Fig. 15, position 1. The clip should not be screwed directly over the tube, but a rubber collar should be placed between clip and tube. Bends in the capillary tube should not have a sharper radius than 35 mm (1 3/8"). In order to prevent vibration there should be an additional support for the tube between the instrument and the engine. Position 2 in Fig. 15 shows a clip placed near the sensing element. The clip should be of such dimensions that it resists vibration and can easily be secured to a cylinder head bolt.

CARBURETTOR

The engine is fitted with a Solex updraught carburettor of flame proof design. The carburettor has a choke control with one air intake; this is used for idling, atomizing and chamber venting. The mouth of the air intake being fitted with a double gauze flame trap.

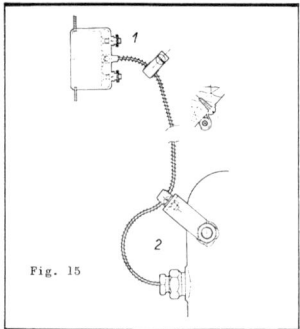

Fig. 15

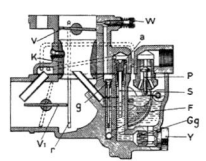

Fig. 16 Section through Solex carburettor.

a Correction jet
F Float
Gg Main jet
g Pilot jet
K Choke tube
P Needle valve
r Excess fuel suction tube
S Atomizing tube
V Throttle butterfly
V_1 Choke (strangler)
W Mixture control for idling
Y Main jet carrier

Idling

The pilot jet, g, with extension pipe, feeds fuel to the engine at low revolutions. The mixture adjustment screw, W, makes possible an exact adjustment of the fuel/air mixture at low speeds. The idling speed of the engine may be adjusted by setting the idling adjustment screw.

Main carburettor

During normal running the engine is fed with fuel through the main jet, Gg, whilst air enters via the choke tube, K, (retained in position by a screw). The richness of the mixture is determined by an air intake, the size of which is governed by the air correction jet, a. Below the air correction jet there is a tube with a number of holes in its sides. This atomizing tube, S, must not be altered or exchanged for a tube of any other type.

Float chamber

The level of the fuel in the float chamber is governed by the hinged double float, F, which actuates the needle valve, P, thus opening or closing the fuel supply hole. This arrangement ensures a regular and constant fuel level and thereby a correct supply to the engine at angles of tilt up to 35^0 in any direction.

Excess fuel suction tube

When the engine is run at low revolutions, it can happen that excess fuel collects in the carburettor air intake. To prevent leakage of this fuel a suction tube, r, is provided. The lower end of this reaches to the lowest point in the air intake and the upper end is connected to the induction pipe above the throttle.

Choke (strangler)

When starting a cold engine, close the choke to ensure a richer fuel mixture. The choke is controlled by a lever attached to the choke spindle. The lever can be remotely controlled by means of the choke cable.

Drain cock

At the lower part of the float chamber there is a drain cock. This is to allow draining of contaminated fuel. When changing fuel the remains of the former fuel should be drained through this cock.

Fuel filter

It is recommended to fit a fuel filter in the supply line from the tank to engine. A filter fitted is a safeguard against foreign bodies and/or water finding its way to the carburettor. When two fuel tanks are fitted for engines running on petrol/paraffin (gasoline/kerosene) then two filters should be installed, one in each fuel line. Remember to clean the filters at regular intervals.

ELECTRICAL SYSTEM

Magneto ignition (engines 0-11 and 0-11 Combi)

Magneto

The engine is fitted with a magneto with a built-in impulse starter of SEM manufacture. The magneto has a rotating permanent magnet which is cast in one piece with the magnet poles and the spindle ends and forms the magneto rotor. The sensitive parts such as the windings and condenser are stationary. The contact breaker is also stationary and of the same construction as a car engine distributor which is fully enclosed in a metal cover.

Ignition timing

A timing lever, A, is fitted to the contact breaker housing (fig. 17). If the timing lever is moved as far as possible in the direction of rotation of the distributor shaft (anti-clockwise), retarded ignition is obtained. If it is moved in the other direction (clockwise), advanced ignition results.

Short-circuiting device

The magneto is fitted with a spring-loaded short-circuiting push button C fig. 17. Depression of the button short-circuits the primary current and thus cuts off the ignition and stops the engine. Short-circuiting of the primary current can also be accomplished by a wire to the body of the engine, connected to a terminal screw D on the magneto cover.

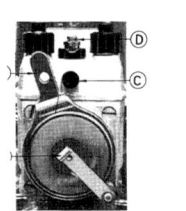

Fig. 17 Magneto for O-11 and O-11 Combi

A Timing lever
B Spring clip
C Short-circuiting button
D Terminal screw

Care and maintenance

The magneto requires little attention as a rule but a periodical inspection is recommended, e.g. when the engine is overhauled.

Lubrication

The ball bearings in the magneto are supplied from the makers ready filled with special grease, which does not require renewal for several years. Cleaning the ball bearings and recharging them with grease should preferably be done by a specialist. Ball bearing grease with a high melting point should be used.

Replacing the ignition lead

If cracks, or other damage, are seen in the insulation of an ignition lead, this should be replaced by a new lead.

1 Unscrew the magneto cover nut for lead outlet.
2 Pull out the ignition lead.
3 Do not bare the new lead. Cut it at right-angles.
4 Push the rubber bushing at least 40 mm ($1\frac{1}{2}$") on to the lead.
5 Press the lead into the high-tension connection as fas as it will go.
6 Refit and tighten the cover nut for the lead outlet, which will draw the rubber bushing into the right position.

Contact breaker

The contact breaker must be checked from time to time. If the points are not clean they should be polished with a fine file, or if one is not available, then with fine emery cloth. Check afterwards that no filings or metal dust remain between the points or in the housing. Final cleaning may be done with a petrol-dampened cloth. The contact gap should be 0.4 mm (0.016"). A feeler gauge is provided on the adjustment spanner for checking this.

When adjusting the contact breaker slacken the screw A, fig 18, but not so much that the contact plate B can move from its position. Set the screwdriver head of the adjustment spanner in the groove C and turn to the left or the right according to whether greater or less gap is required. After adjustment, tighten screw A.

If the spindle cam is removed from the rotor shaft for any reason, check carefully when replacing that it is correctly positioned. The R-marked flat is to be drawn towards the breaker cover.

If the breaker arm D must be replaced, slacken the nut F with the spanner and remove the retaining spring G. The lubrication groove on the breaker spindle should be filled with ball bearing grease before setting the new arm in place.

Apply a few drops of engine oil to the felt pad H if it becomes dry. If entire breaker housing K is replaced, fill the lubrication groove of the new housing with ball bearing grease before fitting.

If the condenser must be replaced, slacken nut F and the retaining screw wich is under the magneto top cover.

Ignition timing adjustments

The magneto is correctly timed at the factory. If the magneto has been removed from the engine and must be retimed when fitted, proceed as follows:

1 Set the piston of cylinder No. 1 (farthest from flywheel) at top dead centre and check that both valves are closed.
2 Set the timing lever to retarded position.
3 Remove the breaker cover.
4 Hold the ignition lead for the sparking plug of cylinder No. 1 some millimeter (a sixteenth of an inch) from the body of the magneto. Turn the driving spindle in its normal direction of rotation until a spark is seen. Check now which of the distributor cams is touching the breaker arm contact. Turn the

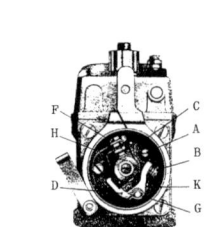

Fig. 18 A Screw
B Contact plate
C Adjustment groove
D Breaker arm
F Nut
G Retaining spring
H Oiled felt pad
K Breaker housing

magneto upside down, thus disconnecting the impulse starter. Turn the driving spindle in its normal direction of rotation until the contact breaker is just open from the cam against which the breaker contact previously rested when the spark was noticed.

5   Turn the magneto the right way up, set it in place, and secure.
6   Refit the breaker cover.
7   Fine adjustment of the ignition must be done when the engine is running at full throttle and is well warmed-up, with normal cooling water temperature. The timing lever should then be set to the advanced position.
8   Slacken the magneto retaining nuts a little so that the magneto can be turned. (Turning is facilitated by the oval bolt holes in the magneto.)
9   Set the magneto in the position that gives maximum engine revolutions without causing knocking.
10 Tighten the magneto retaining nuts.

Coil ignition
(Engines 0-21, 0-21 Combi, 0-41 and 0-411)

This system involves three main components: Battery, ignition coil and distributor. When the ignition is switched on and the contact breaker pionts closed the coil primary winding is energised by a low-tension current from the battery and sets up a powerful magnetisation of the core. As soon as the contact points open, the primary current ceases and, simultaneously, the magnetic field collapses. This generates a powerful high-tension surge in the coil secondary winding, which is passed through the distributor to the spark plug, where a spark is caused. Injurious sparking at the contact breaker is prevented by a condenser in parallel.

Distributor
The distributor is provided with automatic advance mechanism.

Lubrication of distributor
Every 150 hours:
1 Lubricate distributor spindle bearing by screwing down grease cup on distributor body one turn. Refill with Bosch Ft lv 22 grease or equivalent.
2 Lubricate worm in distributor gear housing by screwing down grease cup on housing one turn. Use Shell R 175 or equivalent.

Replacing breaker contacts
1 Smear a very thin layer of grease on the cam surface. Apply a little grease on the rivet side of the breaker lifter and also smear the breaker contact spring lightly. Use Bosch Ft lv 4 grease or equivalent.
2 Lightly grease the breaker arm bushing and bearing pin. After reassembly fill the hollow space above the pin with grease. Use Bosch Ft lv 22 grease or equivalent.
3 Pack the hollow space in the spindle under the distributor rotor with Bosch Ft lv 8 grease or equivalent.

During general overhauls
Send the distributor to a specialist for inspection and adjustment as well as lubrication of among other things the distributor regulator. N.B. Do not allow grease to come in contact with distributor contact points.

Distributor contact breaker
Check the contact breaker frequently. If the points are not clean, polish them with a fine file. Check afterwards that no filings or dust remains between the points. Final cleaning may be done with a petrol-dampened cloth.
Contact gap should be 0.4 mm (0.016") and may be checked with the feeler gauge. To adjust, slacken off screw 3 (fig. 19) slightly and turn adjustment screw 1 to left or right, for greater or less gap as required. After adjustment retighten screw 3 properly. If contact plate 2 has to be replaced, remove screw 3. Partial unscrewing of nut 5 permits removal of the breaker arm 4. Always recheck contact gap after replacement of the breaker arm and the contact plate.

Distributor adjustment
When delivered from the manufacturers the distributor is correctly adjusted. However, after removal from the engine the distributor will require readjustment when replaced. Do this as follows:

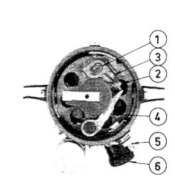

Fig. 19   1 Adjustment screw
          2 Contact plate
          3 Locking screw
          4 Breaker arm
          5 Locking nut
          6 Grease cup

1. Turn engine to bring No. 1 piston (farthest from flywheel) to top dead centre and check that both valves are closed.
2. Remove distributor cover.
3. Turn distributor spindle in normal direction of rotation until contact breaker starts to open, at the same time as the distributor rotor arm points to the ignition contact in the cover. This is distinguished on the outside of the cover by a vertical line beside the ignition lead connection. (The ignition lead from this terminal is connected to No. 1 cylinder spark plug.)
4. Locate distributor in position and secure.
5. Fit distributor cover.
6. Connect ignition leads for firing order 1 - 2 - 4 - 3, i.e. the lead from the marked terminal is connected to No. 1 cylinder spark plug; lead 2, whose contact point is the next in sequence passed by the breaker arm when the engine turns in its normal direction of rotation, is connected to No. 2 cylinder spark plug; lead from connection 3 is connected to No. 4 cylinder spark plug; and the lead from connection 4 is connected to No. 3 cylinder spark plug.
7. Final checking of the ignition must be performed with the engine running under full load, properly warmed to normal cooling water temperature. Slacken the distributor retaining bolts slightly to permit turning of the unit.
8. Turn distributor to the position at which the engine gives maximum r.p.m. without knocking.

(Ignition is advanced by turning the distributor housing in opposite direction of rotation of the distributor spindle and retarded by turning the distributor housing in normal direction of rotation of the distributor spindle.) Finally, tighten the distributor retaining bolts.

Battery

Keep the battery terminals and the terminal clamps free from oxidation and dirt. It is advisable to smear these parts with consistent grease. Check the electrolyte level every week during warm weather, and every second week during cold weather. The correct level is about 10 mm (just under 1/2") over the battery plates. Use only distilled water for topping-up.

Secure the battery absolutely firmly in the boat, bearing in mind sea motion. Place the battery in a well-ventilated position.

Spark plug

Clean the spark plugs at regular intervals, also checking the spark gap. This should be 0.6 mm (0.024") at magneto ignition and 0.7 mm (0.028") at coil ignition.

20

Fig. 20 Wiring diagram

B Wiring diagram for engine with coil ignition, electric equipment and switch box Bosch SH/KSA 1/5.

C Wiring diagram for engine with magneto ignition, dynastarter and switch box Bosch SH/KSA 1/5.

D Wiring diagram for engine with coil ignition, dynastarter and switch box Bosch SH/KSA 1/5.

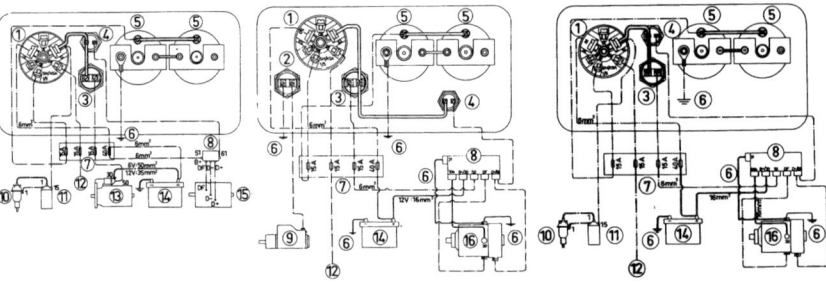

1. Switch box
2. Stop button
3. Starter button
4. Charging control light
5. Instrument lighting
6. Engine body
7. Fuse box
8. Current limit relay
9. Magneto
10. Distributor
11. Ignition coil
12. Connection for lights
13. Starter motor
14. Battery
15. Dynamo
16. Dynastarter

Cable cross-section area should be 2.5 mm^2 (0.004 sq.in.) if not otherwise stated. If cable length exceeds 5 m (16.4 feet) larger area should be used. When relay is mounted on dynamo, cables between relay and dynamo are excluded.

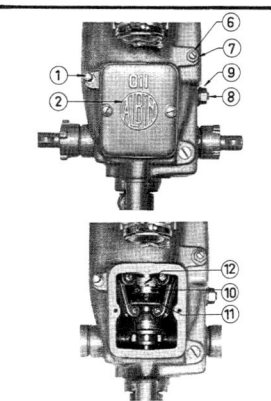

Fig. 21
1 Oil dipstick
2 Inspection cover
6 Adjustment screw for brake band
7 Locking nut
8 Adjustment screw for neutral
9 Locking nut
10 Adjustment nut
11 Stop screw
12 Locking washer

Dynastarter, starter and dynamo

These electric components do not normally require attention. However, these items can with advantage be lubricated and checked by a specialist firm, either every second year or when the engine is overhauled.

The tension of the V-belts should be checked at regular intervals. When tensioned correctly, it should be possible to press in the V-belts about 5 mm (3/16") midway between the flywheel and dynamo belt pulley.

On engines with starter and dynamo special grease should be applied to the starter ring of the flywheel once a year. Use Bosch Ft lv 13 grease or equivalent.

REVERSE GEAR

Lubrication

The oil quantity of the reverse gear for the different engines are: 0-11 and 0-21 1 litre (1.76 Imp.pints, 2.1136 US pints), 0-41 and 0-411 1.7 litres (3 Imp.pints, 3.6 US pints). On engines 0-11 and 0-21 oil is filled through the inspection opening after removal of the cover. On engines 0-41 and 0-411 oil is filled through a special filler opening. A dipstick is provided for checking the level. Use SAE 30 motor oil both winter and summer. All moving parts in the reverse gear are lubricated by splash lubrication.

With new engines the reverse gear oil must be changed after about 25 hours running, thereafter every 250 hours. The oil can be drained through the plug under the reverse gear casing. Should this be inaccessible, suck out the oil with a suction pump through the inspection opening. N.B. After the winter lay-up the oil must always be changed regardless of how little the oil has been used.

Adjustment of reverse gear - engine types 0-11 and 0-21

Adjustment of brake band

If slipping occurs when running astern, this can be eliminated by adjusting the screw 6 fig. 21.

1 Slacken the locking nut 7.
2 Turn adjustment screw 6 about 1/4 turn to the right.
3 Re-tighten the locking nut 7.

If this adjustment is insufficient, repeat the process.

Adjustment of neutral position

This adjustment should be made when the engine has reached the working temperature. If the propeller shaft rotates with the engine when the control lever is at neutral, proceed as follows:

1 Slacken the locking nut 9, fig. 21.
2 Turn the adjustment screw 8 to the left until the shaft ceases to turn.
3 Tighten the locking nut 9.

Should the shaft rotate against engine rotation, turn the adjustment screw to the right.

Adjustment of plate clutch

If the clutch slips when running ahead, adjust as follows:

1 Remove the inspection cover.
2 Slacken the stop screw 11, fig. 21, until it is clear of the groove in the locking washer 12.
3 Turn the adjustment nut 10 to the right until the stop srew 11 reaches the next groove in the locking washer.
4 Tighten the stop screw 11 hard.
5 Replace the inspection cover.

Adjustment of the nut from one groove to the next is normally sufficient. However, if slipping is very bad then an adjustment of two or three grooves may be necessary.

Adjustment of reverse gear - engine types 0-41 and 0-411

Adjustment of reverse position

Normally the factory adjustment of the reverse position will not require changing, unless the brake band lever has been replaced. If adjustment is required, proceed as follows:

1 Slacken the locking nut 5, fig. 22 (see next page).
2 Turn adjustment screw 4 to secure proper gripping of the operating lever in reverse position.
3 Tighten the locking nut 5.

Adjustment of neutral position

This adjustment should be made when the engine is warm. If the propeller shaft rotates with the engine when the control lever is at neutral, proceed as follows:

1 Slacken the locking nut 9, fig. 22.
2 Turn the adjustment screw 8 to the right until the shaft ceases to turn.
3 Tighten the locking nut 9.

Fig. 22 Reverse gear for O-41 and O-411

1 Oil dipstick
2 Inspection cover
3 Oil filler cap
4 Reverse adjustment screw
5 Locking nut
6 Adjustment screw for brake band
7 Locking nut
8 Neutral adjustment screw
9 Locking nut
10 Adjustment nut
11 Stop screw
12 Locking washer

Should the shaft rotate <u>against</u> engine rotation, turn the adjustment screw to the left.

Adjustment of brake band

If slipping occurs when running astern, this can be eliminated by adjusting screw 6, fig. 22, after removal of oil filler cap.

1 Slacken the locking nut 7.
2 Turn the adjustment screw 6 about 1/4 turn to the right.
3 Tighten the locking nut 7.

If this adjustment is insufficient, repeat the process.

Adjustment of plate clutch

If the clutch slips when running ahead, adjust as follows:

1 Remove the inspection cover.
2 Slacken the stop screw 11, fig. 22, until it is clear of the groove in the locking washer 12.
3 Turn adjustment nut 10 to the right until the stop screw 11 reaches the next groove in the locking washer 12.
4 Tighten the stop screw 11 hard.
5 Replace the inspection cover.

Adjustment of the nut from one groove to the next is normally sufficient. However, if slipping is very bad then an adjustment of two or three grooves may be necessary.

REDUCTION GEAR

Engine types O-41 and O-411

The reduction gear contains about 0.4 litre (0.7 Imp.pints, 0.8 US pints) of oil. Refill through the filler opening after removal of the cap. Check the level with the oil dipstick. Use SAE 30 motor oil in all seasons. With new engines the oil of the reduction gear must be changed after the first 25 hours. Thereafter every 250 hours. Drain the gear box by removing the plug on the underside. If this is inaccessible, suck out the oil with the suction pump through the dipstick hole. N.B. Always change the oil after the winter lay-up, regardless of how little the oil has been used.

RUNNING TROUBLES

Some of the most likely causes.

Failure to start

1 Ignition not switched on.
2 Fuel cock switched off or choked filter.
3 Water in the fuel.
4 Choked carburettor jets.
5 Damp or dirty sparking plug. It is also possible that the gap is incorrect.
6 Oxidised breaker points or incorrect breaker gap.

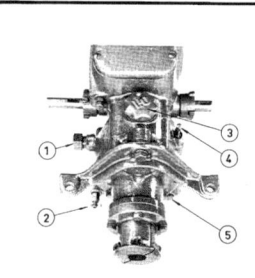

Fig. 23 Reduction gear

1 Cooling water intake
2 Drain cock for cooling water
3 Oil filler cap
4 Oil dipstick
5 Oil drain plug

Sudden stopping

1. Empty fuel tank.
2. Choked fuel tank air vent.
3. Water in the fuel.
4. Dirt or water in the carburettor or in the fuel pipe.
5. Ignition failure.
6. Weak fuel mixture.

Poor performance, uneven running

1. Bad compression due to leaking valves or faulty cylinder head gasket.
2. Too weak, or too rich, fuel mixture.
3. Faulty valve springs. These can have settled.
4. Incorrect valve clearance.
5. Irregular ignition due to a faulty plug, a faulty magneto or distributor.

Knocking

1. Hard or sooty carbon deposits in the combustion space.
2. Excessively advanced ignition.
3. Fuel with too low octane value.
4. Slack piston.
5. Slack connecting rod.

ANTI-CORROSION TREATMENT

for ALBIN marine engines before winter lay-up

During the winter engines run the risk of being damaged by corrosion in the combustion system as well as in the cooling system. It is nearly true to say that a marine engine is never WORN OUT, because of the small number of hours - 200 - 300 a year - that the engine in a normal pleasure boat works. Instead, the engine is worn out gradually by corrosion. Therefore you can radically prolong the life of your engine by giving thorough anti-corrosion treatment in the autumn before laying up the engine for the winter.

Corrosion protection of engine interior

Inner moving parts

1. Preferably decarbonize the engine.
2. Drain motor oil and fill up with anti-corrosive oil (see specification to the right).
3. Empty the fuel tank and clean the whole fuel system.
4. Pour in anti-corrosive fuel sufficient for about one hours running. Suitable mixture is 94-octane petrol (gasoline) and 5% anti-corrosive oil, Albin Motor's part No. 49788.
5. Run the engine for about one hour.

Anti-corrosive oils for inner moving parts

Shell	Ensis Oil 30
Esso	Rust Ban 623
Gulf	Gulf NO-Rust Engine Oil No. 1
Caltex	Preservative Oil 30
BP	Energol Protective Oil 30
Castrol	Castrol Storage Oil
Mobil Oil	Mobil Kote 503
Valvoline	Tectyl 876

Anti-corrosive fluids for cylinder jackets

Shell	Donax C
Esso	Rust Ban 392 (not emulsifying)
Gulf	Gulf Cut 51 A
Caltex	Radiatortex
BP	Soluble Oil EH Energol SB 4
Castrol	Dickool 5 (1/2%)
Mobil Oil	Mobil-Kote 203
Valvoline	Tectyl 81 D Base

Cylinder jackets

1 Drain the cooling water system.

2 Remove the thermostat housing from the cylinder head together with the pipe down front of engine from water pump. With older engines remove the pipe at forward end of engine together with the temperature regulator cock.

3 Plug the cooling water pump outlet, i.e. between the pump and the pipe connected to the cylinder block. Anti-corrosive fluid must not enter the pump.

4 Pour in anti-corrosive fluid through the thermostat hole (or temperature regulator cock) until the whole cooling system is filled. Rubber parts as hoses etc. may be affected by the anti-corrosive fluid.

The cylinder jackets capacity is for 0-11 0.65 litre (1.15 Imp.pints/1.4 US pints), for 0-21 1.25 litres (2.2 Imp.pints/2.7 US pints) and for 0-41 and 0-411 4.7 litres (8.3 Imp.pints/10.0 US pints).

28

Corrosion protection of engine exterior

All unpainted outside surfaces, such as the hot parts of the exhaust pipe, control lever, engine installation bolts etc. should be oiled with a suitable anti-corrosive oil.

Corrosion protection of electrical items

The electrical items are impregnated with lacquer wich perfectly resists storing in a damp and cold atmosphere. Nowadays it is thus not necessary to dismount the electrical equipment from the engine in order to store these parts in a warm room. On the other hand it is beneficial to grease the contact surfaces with preferably a white vaseline.

With older engine types you should as a rule remove the electrical equipment in order to store it in a warm room.

It is good practice to have the electrical equipment overhauled by a specialist once every two or three years.

When preparing the engine for use again

Draw off the anti-corrosive fluid from the cylinder jackets and fit the thermostat (or temperature regulator cock) and all connections. Fill with the recommended lubricating oil and fuel in the usual way and then the engine is ready to be run.

Anti-corrosive oils for outside corrosion protection

Shell	Ensis Fluid 254 or 256
Esso	Rust Ban 395 or Rust Ban 392 (obtainable in spray bottle)
Gulf	NO-Rust 3
Caltex	Rustproof Compound L
BP	Energol Rust Preventive Compound
Castrol	Castrol AR (spray bottle)
Mobil Oil	Mobil-Kote 503
Valvoline	Tectyl 506 (spray bottle)

TECHNICAL DATA	O-11	O-21	O-41	O-411
Number of cylinders	1	2	4	4
Cycle	4-stroke	4-stroke	4-stroke	4-stroke
Bore	78 mm 3.07"	78 mm 3.07"	78 mm 3.07"	78 mm 3.07"
Stroke	92 mm 3.62"	92 mm 3.62"	92 mm 3.62"	92 mm 3.62"
Cylinder capacity	0.44 litres 27 cu.in.	0.88 litres 54 cu.in.	1.76 litres 107 cu.in.	1.76 litres 107 cu.in.
Compression ratio				
Petrol (gasoline) version	5.6:1	5.6:1	5.6:1	6.5:1
Paraffin (kerosene) version	4.8:1	4.8:1	4.8:1	5.0:1
Compression at full throttle and 200 rpm (starter rpm)				
Petrol (gasoline) version	6 kg/cm^2 85 psi	6 kg/cm^2 85 psi	6 kg/cm^2 85 psi	7 kg/cm^2 100 psi
Paraffin (kerosene) version	5 kg/cm^2 71 psi	5 kg/cm^2 71 psi	5 kg/cm^2 71 psi	5.3 kg/cm^2 75 psi
Maximum torque				
Petrol (gasoline) version	2.31 mkg 1300 rpm	4.65 mkg 1400 rpm	9.25 mkg 1300 rpm	11.81 mkg 2000 rpm
Paraffin (kerosene) version	1.93 mkg 1300 rpm	3.58 mkg 1300 rpm	7.82 mkg 1300 rpm	8.65 mkg 1900 rpm
Output at 1600 rpm (O-411 2500 rpm)				
Petrol (gasoline) version	6 SAE hp	12 SAE hp	24 SAE hp	42 SAE hp
Paraffin (kerosene) version	5 SAE hp	10 SAE hp	21 SAE hp	32 SAE hp
Fuel consumption at 1400 rpm (O-411 2500 rpm)				
Petrol (gasoline) version	235 g/bhp/h 0.52 lb	240 g/bhp/h 0.53 lb	240 g/bhp/h 0.53 lb	235 g/bhp/h 0.52 lb
Paraffin (kerosene) version	260 g/bhp/h 0.57 lb	260 g/bhp/h 0.57 lb	260 g/bhp/h 0.57 lb	285 g/bhp/h 0.64 lb
Tappet clearance with cold engine				
Inlet valve	0.20 mm 0.008"	0.20 mm 0.008"	0.20 mm 0.008"	0.20 mm 0.008"
Exhaust valve	0.25 mm 0.010"	0.25 mm 0.010"	0.25 mm 0.010"	0.25 mm 0.010"

	O-11	O-21	O-41	O-411
Oil capacity, engine	0.5 litre 0.9 Imp.pints 1.0 US pints	1.4 litres 2.5 Imp.pints 3.0 US pints	3.3 litres 5.8 Imp.pints 7.0 US pints	5.0 litres 8.8 Imp.pints 10.6 US pints
Oil pressure with warm engine	1.5-2.5 kg/cm^2 20-35 psi	1.5-2.5 kg/cm^2 20-35 psi	1.5-2.5 kg/cm^2 20-35 psi	2.0-3.0 kg/cm^2 28-42 psi
Oil capacity, reverse gear	1.0 litre 1.8 Imp.pints 2.1 US pints	1.0 litre 1.8 Imp.pints 2.1 US pints	1.7 litre 3.0 Imp.pints 3.6 US pints	1.7 litre 3.0 Imp.pints 3.6 US pints
Oil quality	Service MM	Service MM	Service MM	Service MM
Oil viscosity				
above +5° C (40° F)	SAE 30	SAE 30	SAE 30	SAE 30
below +5° C (40° F)	SAE 20	SAE 20	SAE 20	SAE 20
Ignition system	Magneto	Battery	Battery	Battery
Magneto, SEM	EY-1R 33	-	-	-
Distributor, Bosch	-	ZV 2/61 Q1	VE 4 CR 300	VE 4 CR 300
Contact breaker gap	0.4 mm 0.016"	0.4 mm 0.016"	0.4 mm 0.016"	0.4 mm 0.016"
Spark plug, Bosch	M 45 T 1	M 45 T 1	M 45 T 1	M 145 T 1
Spark gap	0.6 mm 0.024"	0.7 mm 0.028"	0.7 mm 0.028"	0.7 mm 0.028"
Electric system	12 Volt	12 Volt	12 Volt	12 Volt
Carburettor, Solex	26 VBN	26 VBN	26 VBN	B*) 32 NV F*) 26 VBN
Carburettor setting				
Choke tube	53455/M/20	53455/M/20	B) 53455/M/18 F) 53455/M/20	B)51708/2/25 F) -
Main jet	50552/1/85	50552/1/90	B) 50552/1/95 F) 50552/1/100	B) 50552/1/140 F) 50552/1/120
Correction jet	51612/180	51612/170	51612/165	B) 51612/210 F) 51612/165
Pilot jet	56004/40	56004/40	B) 56004/45 F) 56004/40	B) 56004/55 F) 56004/45
Emulsion tube	52684/16	52684/16	52684/24	B) 52684/17 F) 52684/24
Needle valve	52844/1.5	52844/1.5	52844/1.5	52844/1.5
Float	53559/9.1 g	53559/9.1 g	53559/9.1 g	53559/9.1 g

*) B = Petrol (gasoline) version, F = Paraffin (kerosene) version

LIST OF CONTENTS

STARTING AND RUNNING	Running-in	6
	Before starting	6
	Starting	7
	After starting	7
	Manoeuvring	7
	Running	7
	Stopping	8
	Special instructions for O-11 Combi and O-21 Combi	8
MAINTENANCE SCHEME		10
LUBRICATING SYSTEM		11
COOLING SYSTEM		12
CARBURETTOR		13
ELECTRICAL SYSTEM	Magneto ignition (O-11 and O-11 Combi)	15
	Coil ignition (O-21, O-21 Combi, O-41 and O-411)	18
	Battery	20
	Spark plug	20
	Wiring diagram	21
	Dynastarter, starter and dynamo	22
REVERSE GEAR	Lubrication	22
	Adjustment of reverse gear, O-11 and O-21	23
	Adjustment of reverse gear, O-41 and O-411	23
REDUCTION GEAR		25
RUNNING TROUBLES		25
ANTI-CORROSION TREATMENT		27
TECHNICAL DATA		30

The specifications and design information given in this book are not binding. We reserve the right to carry out modifications without previous notice.

ALBIN

INSTRUCTION MANUAL No 1125 E
Reverse gear 0-11 and 0-21

Dismantling and reassembly of reverse gear for ALBIN marine engines 0-11 and 0-21

If the reverse gear for any reason must be dismantled and reassembled proceed according to the following instruction which applies to engines both with and without raised rear crank start.

Dismantling

Points 5, 6, 7, 8, and 16 apply only to engines with raised rear crank start. The instructions are otherwise similar for engines both with and without raised rear crank start.

1. Drain oil from reverse gear casing.
2. Release the shaft coupling 1 (Fig. 1) with the propeller shaft.
3. Unscrew nut 2 and remove the Waller washer, 3.
4. Unscrew bolt 7 and remove the coupling half, 6. (The washer, 4, and the sealing ring, 5, will accompany the coupling half.)
5. Remove the cover from the start crank pillar A (Fig. 2).
6. Slacken the four bolts which secure the pillar to the case and lower the pillar until the chain is released from the sprockets B and C.
7. Remove the cover D from the gear wheel E and knock out the tubular pin F.
8. Draw out shaft G aft and remove the gear wheel E.
9. Remove the retainer, 8, (Fig. 1) from the ball bearing, 10, and knock out the key, 9.
10. Remove the inspection cover and the dipstick.
11. Slacken the four bolts, 20, which secure the reverse gear casing 16 to the cylinder block. N.B. Where raised crank start is fitted one of these bolts is located inside the casing, 16. This bolt can be removed via the opening for the gear wheel, E in Fig. 2.
12. Put the control lever to forward and, if necessary, tap the projecting control lever shaft, 13, with a lead hammer or similar tool so that the casing, 16, is shifted slightly away from the cylinder block. N.B. Strike the shaft itself, not the sealing ring retainer.
13. Move the lock washer, 11, to the rear and unscrew the adjustment nut, 12. Then place the control lever in neutral.
14. The casing, 16, can now be fully removed by tapping towards aft on the control lever shaft, 13. (The ball bearing 10, lock washer, 11, adjustment nut, 12, cone, 15, and the brake band will follow with the casing, 16.)
15. The gear housing can be removed after unbolting the split securing collar, 18. Be careful to remove the dowel pin, 19, from the shaft.
16. Slacken the two screws, I in Fig. 2, and remove the gear wheel, H.

Refitting

Points 1, 9, 10, 11, 12, and 13 refer only to engines with raised crank start. Otherwise, the instructions apply to engines both with and without raised crank start.

1. Fit the gear wheel, H, with its pawl, K, Fig. 2. Turn the gear wheel so that the pawl is at its lower position and so that a line through the two screws, I, would be horizontal, as shown in Fig. 2.
2. Fit the key, 17, Fig. 1, and set the gear housing in position. The gear housing is secured by the collar, 18. Check that the dowel pin, 19, is fully entered into the shaft hole. Where raised crank start is fitted see that the pawl, K, in Fig. 2, is free from the shoulders of the collar, 18, when at its lower position.
3. Dismantle the ball bearing, 10, from the reverse gear casing, 16, and place the cone, 15, in the control fork end, 14. In the event of any change in the brake band adjustment, check that the band is not too tightly adjusted when the reverse gear casing is lifted into place.

4. With the control lever in neutral, set the reverse gear casing, 16, in place. (Check the gasket between the casing and the cylinder block.)

5. Screw in the four bolts, 20, remembering that the short bolt (shown in Fig. 1) shall be fitted at upper right.

6. Fit the adjustment nut, 12, and the lockwasher, 11. The adjustment nut shall be fitted with the bevelled face aft and shall be threaded on as far as the threading allows. See that no locking lips of the lockwasher are folded down before placing this on the shaft.

7. Fit the ball bearing, 10, and the key, 9.

8. Fit the retainer, 8, and its packing. (Check the sealing ring in the retainer, 8.)

9. Check that the gear wheel, H in Fig. 2, is in the position described in point 1 and shown in Fig. 2.

10. Fit shaft G and sprocket C simultaneously with the placing of gear E. Check that the hole for the tubular pin F comes in such a position (as shown in Fig. 2) that the pin can be fitted without moving the gear wheel, E.

11. Fit the pin, F.

12. Fit the chain over the upper sprocket, B, and set up the pillar, A. The start crank should hang vertically, as in Fig. 2. Pass the chain over the lower sprocket C. The sprocket should then be in the position determined by the previous setting of the gear wheel, H, i.e. the position as shown in Fig. 2.

13. Fit the cover on the pillar, A, and the cover D.

14. Mount coupling 6 (Fig. 1) tight against the ball bearing, 10. Do not tighten the bolt, 7, yet.

15. Fit the sealing, 5, and the washer, 4.

16. Screw on the nut, 2, but not fit the Waller washer, 3.

17. Make sure that the crankshaft is tight against the rear main bearing by knocking the forward crankshaft end a couple of times with a lead hammer. Tighten up nut 2.

18. Place the control lever in forward.

19. Back off the adjustment nut, 12, so that this nut and the washer, 11, lie tight against the ball bearing, 10.

20. Remove nut 2 and slide the coupling half, 6, to the rear a little by tapping it lightly in the aft direction.

21. Back off nut 12 a further 3/4 turn on the shaft and note that one of the grooves in the nut comes exactly opposite one of the locking lips on the lockwasher. Fold down the lip so that the nut is secured. This is easiest done with a small screwdriver.

22. Tap the coupling, 6, lightly once or twice so that it moves forward, tight against the ball bearing, 10. Fit the Waller washer, 3, and tighten up nut 2 properly.

23. Tighten up the bolt, 7.

24. Replace the dipstick and fill the reverse gear casing with oil.

25. Refit the inspection cover. Refit the shaft coupling, 1, when the propeller shaft is re-installed.

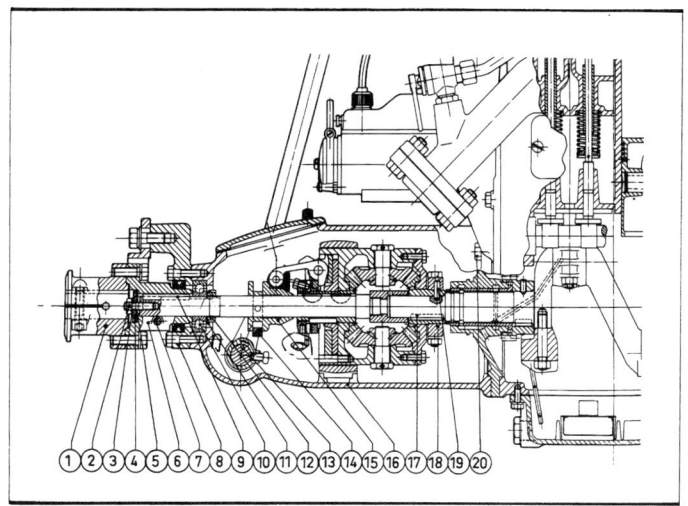

Fig. 1 Section through reverse gear

1 Coupling half for propeller shaft
2 Nut
3 Waller washer
4 Coupling half washer
5 Sealing
6 Coupling half for reverse gear shaft
7 Coupling securing bolt
8 Ball bearing retainer
9 Key
10 Ball bearing
11 Lockwasher
12 Adjustment nut
13 Control lever shaft
14 Control fork end
15 Engagement cone
16 Casing
17 Key
18 Securing collar
19 Dowel pin
20 Screws (4)

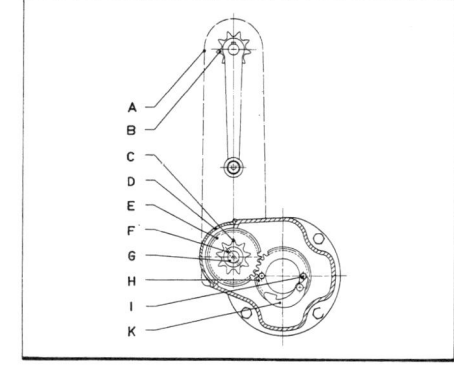

Fig. 2 Raised rear crank start

A Pillar
B Upper sprocket
C Lower sprocket
D Cover for gear wheel
E Gear wheel in cover
F Sprung tubular pin
G Shaft
H Gear wheel with pawl
I Screws (2)
K Pawl